LIFEBOATS

Nicholas Leach

Shire Publica

GW00643776

The lifeboat 'Frank and Marion', which served at the New Quay station in Cardiganshire from 1886 until 1907, at the bottom of the stone slipway inside the shelter of the long stone quay. Until 1904, when a new lifeboat house was built, the lifeboat was hauled up to a boathouse situated above the harbour on the only practicable spot available. A powerful winch was needed as the house was at the top of a long incline. The effort required by the crew and launchers must have been considerable, for not only was the hill long and quite steep, but the house was at right angles to the stone slipway. (RNLI)

CONTENTS

Cover: *The 47 foot (14.3 metre) Tyne class 'City of London' launching down the slipway at Selsey. The lifeboat is held in place in the lifeboat house by retaining chains and a pin. After the chains are removed, the pin is knocked out with a hammer and the lifeboat goes down the slipway, gathering momentum and making an impressive and dramatic sight on hitting the water. (Nicholas Leach)*

ACKNOWLEDGEMENTS

The author and publishers are grateful to the following for their assistance in the preparation of this book: Shelley Woodroffe, RNLI Headquarters, Poole; Peter Bendall, Cambridge; Sarah Ford, Birmingham. The author also expresses his thanks to the crews and officials who have welcomed him at so many lifeboat stations throughout Great Britain and the Republic of Ireland.

British Library Cataloguing in Publication Data: Leach, Nicholas. Lifeboats. – (Shire album; 336). Lifeboat service – Great Britain. 2. Life-boats. 3. Life-boats – History. 4. Lifeboat service – Great Britain – History. I. Title. 363.1'23'81'0941. ISBN 0 7478 0366 8.

Published in 1998 by Shire Publications Ltd, Cromwell House, Church Street, Princes Risborough, Buckinghamshire HP27 9AA, UK. Copyright © 1998 by Nicholas Leach. First published 1998. Shire Album 336. ISBN 0 7478 0366 8.

Nicholas Leach is hereby identified as the author of this work in accordance with Section 77 of the Copyright, Designs and Patents Act 1988.

All rights reserved. No part of this publication may be reproduced or transmitted in any form or by any means, electronic or mechanical, including photocopy, recording, or any information storage and retrieval system, without permission in writing from the publishers.

Printed in Great Britain by CIT Printing Services, Press Buildings, Merlins Bridge, Haverfordwest, Pembrokeshire SA61 1XF.

Left: *An engraving of the life-boat built by Henry Great-head at South Shields, the first boat to be designed and built specifically to save lives at sea. This illustration appeared in 1802, entitled 'A Perspective View of Mr Great-head's Boat Going to Assist a Ship in Distress'. It was drawn from a model presented by Greathead to the Admiralty and clearly shows the construction and hull form of the boats he built, characterised by the curved keel.*

Right: *A diagrammatic repre-sentation and cross-section of Greathead's lifeboat, and the small carriage on which it was intended to transport the boat.*

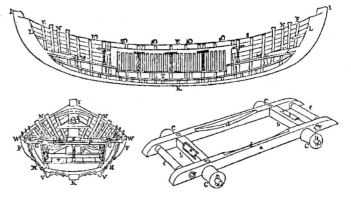

THE FIRST COASTAL LIFESAVERS

The seas around the coasts of the United Kingdom and the Republic of Ireland are some of the most treacherous waters anywhere in the world. Yet, as island nations, Britain and Ireland have for centuries been dependent on using those waters for trade and commerce and also, in the last few decades, for pleasure. The dangers faced by those going to sea have been met by a humane spirit of compassion and charity that is rarely matched in other walks of life. The lifeboat service is perhaps the best example of this spirit: the crews that man the boats have always been volunteers. For no personal gain, they are prepared to go to sea to save the lives of others, often in the worst weather. This combination of selflessness and courage has for well over a century made lifeboat crews special in the eyes of the public.

Britain has a strong tradition of saving life at sea, and the Royal National Lifeboat Institution (RNLI) is justifiably proud of its long history. The lifeboat service of Britain and Ireland is dedicated to continuing this tradition and operates some of the best lifeboats ever built – advanced craft that are strong, seaworthy, fast and technologically impressive.

Although it is difficult to establish with certainty when and where lifesaving at sea began, the first recorded attempts to place lifeboats on the coast were made during the last quarter of the eighteenth century, when the industrial revolution was gathering momentum. Before this time the remedies for shipwrecks had not included the building of a boat specifically designed to be operated from the shore and used to save those in distress at sea. Navigational aids, such as lighthouses, had been built at strategic points to assist ships, but no concerted efforts had been made to improve the passage of ships around the coast.

The foundations of Britain's lifeboat service were laid during the fifty years from the 1770s to the 1820s. As industrial output expanded, the number of ships carrying cargoes around the coasts increased. These were sailing vessels reliant solely on wind power and so were at the mercy of storms and gales; wrecks were frequent, and crews and valuable cargoes were often lost as a result. From the 1770s there was mounting concern about such losses, and the need became acute to have a suitable boat on shore ready to put out to sea to aid vessels in distress.

The 'Two Sisters', seen in the 1860s on her launching carriage outside the boathouse where she was kept, was the first lifeboat to serve the Ramsey station on the Isle of Man. The founder of the RNLI, Sir William Hillary, lived on the Isle of Man and was closely connected with the lifeboat at Douglas. Although he made great efforts to obtain lifeboats for the Isle of Man during the 1820s and 1830s, it was not until the second half of the nineteenth century that the RNLI began to fund and operate lifeboats on the island. (RNLI)

The first recorded lifeboat was at Formby, where it served the entrance to the river Mersey; it was set up and financed by the Liverpool Docks Commissioners and began operation in the 1770s. We do not know the name of the boat or other details. As the fastest growing port on the west coast, Liverpool had great need of lifeboat protection, and the Commissioners funded another boat, which was placed at Hoylake in 1803.

On the east coast the fastest growing port was Newcastle upon Tyne, and the first boat known to have been designed and built specifically for lifesaving had its origins in that city. It was built by Henry Greathead in 1790 at South Shields, on the south bank of the mouth of the river Tyne, and operated from there for several decades. The impetus to design, build and operate this lifeboat was provided by the loss of the collier *Adventure* at South Shields. The *Adventure* was one of a fleet of colliers that got into difficulty when approaching the mouth of the Tyne. Most of the colliers succeeded in reaching the safety of the harbour, but the *Adventure* was doomed and is said to have 'exhibited such a picture of distress as cannot be described'. She lay in shallow water until her anchor broke, causing her to run aground close to shore, and the master and seven men perished.

The growing awareness of ship losses among shipowners and underwriters prompted greater efforts to reduce the dangers to life, ships and trade. A

4

second boat was built by Greathead in 1798 and stationed at North Shields. During the first decade of the nineteenth century Lloyd's insurance agency set up a fund that encouraged the building and operating of lifeboats to counter ship losses. This fund provided an impetus to early lifeboat building and helped pay for almost thirty lifeboats up to the 1820s. Yet, despite this assistance from Lloyd's in London, the establishment of lifeboat stations was still somewhat fragmented and involved essentially local arrangements, with local funding. There was neither co-ordination of lifeboat stations nor lifeboat building on a national basis until well into the nineteenth century.

THE EARLY YEARS OF THE RNLI

In 1823 Sir William Hillary, of Douglas in the Isle of Man, wrote and published 'An Appeal to the British Nation on the Humanity and Policy of Forming a National Institution for the Preservation of Lives and Property from Shipwreck', setting out his ideas for forming a national body whose sole responsibility would be the preservation of human life from shipwreck.

At a meeting in London on 4th March 1824, the Royal National Institution for the Preservation of Life from Shipwreck was founded, mainly as a result of Sir William's efforts. Initially it was quite successful, and the new organisation added to the number of lifeboats in operation, but from the 1830s it started to falter through lack of funds. Annual income dwindled further during the 1840s and reached its lowest level by 1850, no public appeals having been made for over a decade. Reform of the Institution was essential if it was to continue its work.

The large 42 foot self-righter 'Edmund Harvey' (right) and the smaller lifeboat 'Arab' afloat in Padstow harbour, Cornwall, in the early twentieth century. Many stations operated two lifeboats, usually a large boat for deep-water work offshore and a smaller one for casualties closer inshore. This practice was gradually phased out with the introduction of the motor lifeboat in the 1920s and 1930s. This postcard shows the two Padstow lifeboats afloat for demonstration purposes, and two drogues can be seen on the stern end boxes of the 'Edmund Harvey'. (Photo by a Shoreline member)

There are many memorials to lifeboatmen whose lives have been lost while going to the service of others. The three on this page commemorate major lifeboat disasters and are moving reminders of the power of the sea and of the bravery and courage of lifeboatmen. Right: *This memorial at Burrow near Wexford, Ireland, was erected in 1981 to commemorate the exploits of the lifeboatmen from Rosslare who went to help the Norwegian schooner 'Mexico', which was wrecked in February 1914. Four lifeboats went to the aid of the schooner, one of which, the Fethard lifeboat 'Helen Blake', was capsized, with the loss of nine lifeboatmen. There is a memorial to those men in the centre of Fethard village. (Nicholas Leach)*

In December 1849 there was a disaster at the mouth of the Tyne when one of the local society's lifeboats capsized within sight of land, with the loss of twenty of the twenty-four men on board. The fourth Duke of Northumberland, then First Lord of the Admiralty, became President of the Institution in 1851, and it was evident to him that reform was urgently needed. Under his guidance, during the early 1850s, the service was reformed and reorganised.

It was clear also that a new design of lifeboat was essential. After consulting the Chairman and Deputy Chairman of the Institution in May 1850, the Duke drew up a prospectus for a

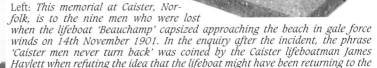

Left: *This memorial at Caister, Norfolk, is to the nine men who were lost when the lifeboat 'Beauchamp' capsized approaching the beach in gale force winds on 14th November 1901. In the enquiry after the incident, the phrase 'Caister men never turn back' was coined by the Caister lifeboatman James Haylett when refuting the idea that the lifeboat might have been returning to the beach. (Nicholas Leach)*

This memorial on the sea front at St Anne's, Lancashire, commemorates the lifeboatmen lost going to the aid of a German barque, also called 'Mexico', on 9th December 1886. St Anne's, Lytham and Southport lifeboats all went to the barque. The Southport lifeboat was launched first, but as she attempted to veer down on the ship she was struck by heavy seas and capsized with the loss of all but two of her crew. The St Anne's boat was also lost, under sail, though the precise details of her fate are not known other than that her entire crew of thirteen were lost. This double tragedy was the worst disaster in the RNLI's history. (Nicholas Leach)

6

national competition to test the ideas of boatbuilders and designers throughout the nation. Out of the 282 plans submitted, the winning design was by James Beeching, a Great Yarmouth boatbuilder. His boat was self-righting; a low waist and high aircases at each end caused it to come upright in the event of a capsize.

Beeching built several boats to his design, which was subsequently modified and improved, under the instructions of the Institution, by James Peake, Master Shipwright of the Royal Naval Dockyard at Woolwich. Peake's design of self-righter was altered and improved over time and eventually became the accepted lifeboat type throughout Britain, except on the coasts of East Anglia, where a larger type was more suitable for local conditions.

In 1854 the Institution, whose old title was often shortened to the 'National Shipwreck Institution', was renamed the Royal National Lifeboat Institution, which was deemed more appropriate and also more accurate. Most of the local lifeboat associations, responsible for only one or two stations, were absorbed by the renamed body. This process continued as the national organisation expanded its operations throughout the second half of the nineteenth century.

The maximum number of lifeboats in operation was reached in 1895, when there were 308 RNLI lifeboats around the coast. This was in the heyday of the 'standard' self-righting lifeboat, which had been improved over the years. By the 1880s it was almost the only type of lifeboat in service and was used widely throughout the world. It was primarily a rowing boat, only 34 feet (10.4 metres) or 35 feet (10.7 metres) in length, and its range of action was limited. For this reason, at many stations two lifeboats were operated, and at some, such as Hartlepool and Sunderland, there were no fewer than five boats at one time.

The Scarborough lifeboat going out on service to save the crew of five from the schooner 'Black-Eyed Susan', one of four vessels caught in a severe storm on 28th October 1880. This nineteenth-century print shows the pulling lifeboat 'Lady Leigh' leaving her carriage with the casualty in sight of the beach, breaking up in the heavy surf. Pulling lifeboats did not have a great range, so many were needed to cover the coast, and vessels that were in distress close to land – and a lifeboat station – stood the best chance of being saved. At the time of this rescue there were almost three hundred lifeboat stations, more than at any time before or since. (Illustrated London News)

The self-righting lifeboats used at the RNLI's new stations were often launched from a carriage off an open beach. Because they were light enough to be launched in this way, and because sailing against the wind in a vessel relying solely on manpower was slow and exhausting work, these lifeboats were sometimes taken further afield by land to be launched at a place from which they could reach the casualty more easily.

The lifeboatmen of the nineteenth century performed many heroic and courageous acts using this type of boat. One of the most remarkable rescues, in which the lifeboat was moved overland before being launched, occurred in January 1881 when the brig *Visitor*, carrying coal to London, was grounded in rough weather close to Robin Hood's Bay in North Yorkshire. The nearest lifeboat was at Whitby, but to row the lifeboat several miles to the wreck would have been virtually impossible in the driving snow and huge seas. It was therefore decided to manhandle the lifeboat over 8 miles (13 km) of hills, through fields and snowdrifts, to Robin Hood's Bay for launching. Almost everybody in Whitby helped, and after three hours of concerted effort the lifeboat was launched to the aid of the *Visitor*. Despite the freezing conditions, the lifeboat reached the casualty successfully and all of its crew were saved in a truly extraordinary rescue.

Despite its widespread use and its success in effecting many rescues, the self-righting type of lifeboat had its problems. In order to right in the event of a capsize, it had a relatively narrow beam. This made it less stable than a non-self-righting lifeboat and thus more prone to capsize in the first place. There were a number of accidents, many of them fatal, involving this type of lifeboat throughout the late nineteenth century. One of these, when two lifeboats capsized going to the same vessel, led to a thorough reappraisal of lifeboat design.

On 9th December 1886 the self-righting lifeboats from Lytham, St Anne's and Southport in Lancashire put out to the aid of the German barque *Mexico*, which had been wrecked in the Ribble estuary. With a severe gale blowing, the lifeboats encountered terrible conditions but continued towards the casualty. The Southport lifeboat capsized after having reached the *Mexico* and failed to right, with the loss of fourteen of her sixteen crew. The St Anne's lifeboat capsized some distance from the wreck and also failed to right; her entire crew of thirteen was lost. The upturned boat and the bodies of some of the crew were found washed ashore next day. However, the Lytham lifeboat, despite the huge seas she encountered, got alongside the *Mexico* and took off her entire crew.

Following these tragedies the RNLI re-examined the design of its lifeboats. Among the recommendations of the enquiry into the Ribble disaster was the proposal that the RNLI appoint a Consulting Naval Architect, and George Lennox Watson accepted the post in 1887. Under his guidance, a new design was introduced which sacrificed the self-righting principle in favour of a boat that was larger, steadier and far less likely to capsize under sail. The new type, over 42 feet (12.8 metres) long, was essentially a sailing lifeboat.

The situation was kept constantly under review, and the newly designed Watson sailing lifeboats pointed the way forward for the RNLI. The new type was seen as sophisticated by comparison with the smaller self-righting lifeboats, and as it had a greater radius of action the RNLI began to reduce the number of stations.

Towards the end of the nineteenth century, once the Watson-designed sailing lifeboat had been perfected, the Institution entered a new phase of development, looking at different ways of powering lifeboats. Experiments took place with first steam and later petrol engines, indicating the direction that lifesaving at sea would take in the twentieth century.

The pulling lifeboat 'Elizabeth Leicester', which was stationed at Whitehaven from 1903 to 1925. She was a standard self-righting lifeboat, 34 feet (10.4 metres) in length and rowed by ten men. The crew was thirteen in total, most of whom can be seen on board in their positions, complete with cork life-jackets. Note the drogue at the stern of the boat, which was towed in following seas to smooth the ride in the worst of weathers. This posed photograph shows her outside the boathouse towards the end of her service career. (Reproduced with permission of The Beacon, Whitehaven)

A practice launch of the pulling lifeboat 'Elizabeth Leicester' from the beach at Whitehaven in 1910. Attached to the wheels of the launching carriage are 'Tipping's plates'. These were introduced towards the end of the 1880s and were regarded as an 'invaluable device which has made possible the transporting of heavy lifeboats over deep and soft sand'. (Reproduced with permission of The Beacon, Whitehaven)

The St Helier lifeboat 'William Henry Wilkinson' being hauled from the boathouse. The wheels of the carriage are stuck in the shingle, making the launch problematic. A carriage launch is a complex operation, requiring considerable effort on the part of the launchers, who are as important to the lifeboat stations as the lifeboatmen themselves. (RNLI)

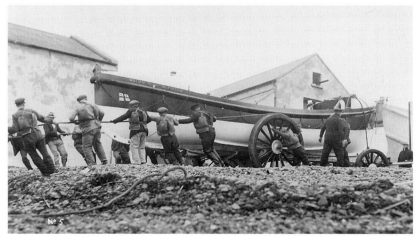

The Hoylake lifeboat 'Hannah Fawsett Bennett' being shown to a group of children on the beach in the early 1900s. The station was established in 1802, but this was the first lifeboat provided by the RNLI after they took control of the station in 1894. At Hoylake when the tide is low the lifeboat has to cross 2 miles (3 km) of sand before reaching a suitable launch site. During the nineteenth century the station was operated by the Mersey Docks and Harbours Board, the forerunners of which provided the first known lifeboat at Formby, at the opposite side of the Mersey entrance to Hoylake. (RNLI)

Some of the first trials with lifeboat-launching tractors were carried out at Hoylake in 1921. Pulling the lifeboat across 2 miles (3 km) of wet sand to the water's edge provided a stern test for the vehicles. The early tractors were relatively primitive; here the reserve motor lifeboat 'Maria Stephenson' is being pulled across the beach by one of the first lifeboat-launching tractors, built by the Four Wheel Drive (FWD) Lorry Company. (RNLI)

The modern lifeboat at Hoylake has to face the same conditions as its predecessors, although with a much more powerful launching tractor less effort is needed on the part of the launchers. For the recovery of the station's lifeboat, the aluminium-hulled Mersey class 'Lady of Hilbre', two tractors are used, one to haul the lifeboat from the water and pull the boat and carriage back to the boathouse, and another to carry the skids used to smooth the lifeboat's passage over the sand. (Nicholas Leach)

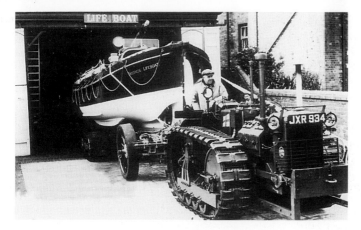

A contemporary postcard showing the Skegness lifeboat 'The Cuttle' and the launching tractor outside the lifeboat house in the 1950s. (Photograph by a Shoreline member)

Tractor trials being carried out at Pwllheli in November 1951 using Case tractor T53 and the reserve lifeboat 'Sir Heath Harrison'. The design of lifeboat-launching tractors gradually improved between the two world wars, and tractors designed by the Case company for agricultural work were adapted by the Roadless Traction Company for use at lifeboat stations. The caterpillar tracks enabled these vehicles to work over most beach conditions. (RNLI)

THE DEVELOPMENT OF THE POWERED LIFEBOAT

During the nineteenth century lifeboatmen using the pulling and sailing lifeboats performed some remarkable and extraordinary feats of lifesaving. Nevertheless, it was obvious that the use of steam power in a lifeboat would offer advantages over a lifeboat relying on sails, oars or a combination of the two, but designing and building a steam-powered lifeboat presented lifeboat designers with a completely different set of problems from those of a pulling lifeboat design. The idea of a steam lifeboat had been discussed since 1825, but all the suggestions that had been put forward were rejected.

However, advances in engineering techniques during the 1880s made the building of a steam-powered lifeboat a possibility, and in 1890 it became a reality when the first steam-powered lifeboat, the *Duke of Northumberland*, was launched from her builder's yard on the Thames and made her first trial trip. During the next decade the RNLI had a further five steam lifeboats built for service around the British Isles. They remained in use for almost three decades and are credited with having saved more than six hundred lives.

These impressive vessels were all over 50 feet (15.2 metres) in length and could cover a much greater area than any pulling or sailing lifeboat. However, their size severely restricted the number of places where they could be stationed. They had to be kept moored afloat, although at this time lifeboats in general were kept afloat only as a last resort because anti-fouling paints were not as effective as they are now. Manning presented difficulties as specialist engineers were required to service the boiler. In addition the boats were not ideal for operation in shallow water.

The steam lifeboat 'James Stevens No.3' and motor lifeboat 'Duke of Connaught', destined for the Baltimore station in southern Ireland, sailing down the river Thames during a publicity trip on 4th August 1919. The RNLI's first steam lifeboat, 50 feet (15.2 metres) long and powered by water-jets, was built in 1889. Only six steam lifeboats were built by the RNLI, although at several stations steam tugs were often employed to tow the pulling lifeboat to sea. Steam was the first motive power to be applied to lifeboats, but at the time of this photograph steam lifeboats were being taken out of service in favour of motor lifeboats. The petrol-driven internal combustion engine, which had been developed to be sufficiently reliable to power lifeboats in the worst of weathers, was a more viable propulsion method. (RNLI)

While steam was poorly suited to power lifeboats, the newly invented internal combustion engine offered greater potential. Petrol-driven engines were developed during the second half of the nineteenth century and first used to power motor vehicles in the 1880s. By the 1900s it was inevitable that motor power, in the form of the internal combustion engine, would become a vital element in lifesaving. In 1904 a lifeboat was fitted with a petrol engine for the first time. Many difficulties had to be overcome in order to operate such an engine successfully on board a lifeboat, but once these technical problems had been solved it was clear that lifeboats powered by the internal combustion engine marked the way ahead.

At first, lifeboats already in service were converted by the fitting of a petrol engine. In 1908 the first lifeboat to be built with an engine was completed, and by 1914 more than ten motor lifeboats were in service. Further advances in design and development were delayed considerably by the First World War of 1914-18. However, following the cessation of hostilities, the RNLI adopted a policy of modernisation which resulted in many new motor lifeboats being built to replace the pulling, sailing and steam lifeboats. In addition, there were several important improvements in the design of the motor lifeboat.

Most lifeboats in the period immediately after the First World War were based on old designs of sailing lifeboats but were fitted with a single engine driving a single propeller. As the RNLI gained greater experience in the operation of motor lifeboats, more reliable engines were developed to power larger boats, which were able to cover greater areas. In the 1920s James Barnett, the RNLI's Consulting Naval Engineer, designed a 60 foot (18.3 metre) lifeboat that employed twin engines and twin propellers, eliminating the need for the auxiliary sails that single-engined motor lifeboats carried. In 1932 a diesel engine was fitted to a lifeboat for the first time.

Like George Watson before him, Barnett believed that greater overall stability was more important than self-righting properties. The lifeboat types that he designed were large twin-engined non-self-righting boats. These boats became the mainstay of the lifeboat fleet for many decades and effected some notable rescues. One of the most courageous was performed on 23rd November 1938 by the New Brighton lifeboat, *William and Kate Johnston*. The endurance of the boat was put to the test when she went to the aid of two casualties, saving three lives from the first and four from the second. In the process the lifeboat sustained serious damage, including three holes in her hull, but this did not impair her seaworthiness. The RNLI's Silver Medal for gallantry was awarded to the coxswain, William Jones, for his skill and

The 61 foot (18.6 metre) Barnett lifeboat 'Princess Mary', stationed at Padstow, moored afloat in the Camel estuary. This type was the first lifeboat to be fitted with two engines and two propellers. When it was introduced in the 1920s it was the largest lifeboat built for the RNLI. Because of its size it had to be moored afloat. This limited the number of stations at which it could operate, and as a result only four boats of this type and size were built, of which the last was the Padstow boat. The other three were slightly shorter, at 60 feet (18.3 metres). (RNLI)

courage in using the power of the boat to full advantage, and Bronze Medals were awarded to three other members of the crew.

By the outbreak of the Second World War almost the whole of the lifeboat fleet had been motorised as a result of the modernisation programme pursued by the RNLI, and only fifteen pulling and sailing boats remained in service. However, although it was relatively well equipped, the RNLI was severely affected by the war. Lifeboats were forced to operate in conditions more hazardous than ever and even routine services were more difficult than in peacetime.

During the war some of the most outstanding rescues and courageous acts ever performed by lifeboat coxswains and crews took place. There was none more courageous than Henry Blogg, the coxswain of the Cromer lifeboat, who is perhaps the most famous lifeboatman of all time. He was awarded the

13

Despite all efforts to provide the most seaworthy lifeboats for service around the coasts of the British Isles, tragedies do occur. The St Ives lifeboat station was hit by two disasters within a single year. On 31st January 1938 the station's first motor lifeboat, the 'Caroline Parsons', went to the aid of the steamer 'Alba'. While returning, she was capsized and wrecked, with the loss of five of those rescued from the steamer, though all the lifeboatmen came ashore alive. The former Padstow lifeboat 'John and Sarah Eliza Stych' was sent as a replacement, but less than a year later she was capsized three times on a rescue. This time, however, the lifeboatmen were not so fortunate and, although the boat righted successfully on each occasion as she was designed to do, seven of the eight crew on board were lost during the capsizes. The lifeboat was eventually thrown ashore at Gwithian, where the sole survivor was able to crawl out and call for help. The damaged lifeboat, as seen in the photograph, was examined on the rocks which were to be her final resting place. (Photograph by a Shoreline member)

The last sailing lifeboat in service, 'William Cantrell Ashley', at New Quay in Cardiganshire. She was replaced in 1948. By the end of the Second World War, the RNLI's fleet consisted almost entirely of motor lifeboats, although it was not until 1957 that the last pulling boat, which was the number two lifeboat at Whitby, was taken out of service. (RNLI)

RNLI's Gold Medal for gallantry, its highest accolade, three times and took part in many spectacular rescues. He commanded the Cromer lifeboat on numerous occasions during the war and helped to save many lives.

At the Humber lifeboat station on Spurn Point, Coxswain Robert Cross performed a service during the war that earned him the RNLI's Gold Medal. In February 1940, on a bitterly cold day, with snow falling and a strong wind blowing, the lifeboat *City of Bradford II* with Cross in command was launched to the aid of the steam trawler *Gurth*, which had struck the shore. Cross brought the lifeboat to the scene, anchored 150 yards (137 metres) from the ship and manoeuvred towards it. Despite heavy seas washing over the lifeboat, Cross was able to bring the boat close enough to the wreck for a few seconds at a time to take off all its crew. In the broken surf, with only one engine working fully, the operation took nearly four hours. This was later described by the RNLI as 'one of the most difficult and gallant rescues in the history of the Lifeboat Service'.

POST-WAR REBUILDING

Although many gallant rescues were performed during the Second World War, lifeboat construction and development had effectively been halted during the war years. After 1945, therefore, there was a need to start building new lifeboats again and the RNLI embarked on a programme of constructing new boats, all of which had twin engines and twin propellers. As the new boats were completed and went on station, the pulling and sailing lifeboats were phased out, but there was nevertheless, in the decades following the Second World War, a number of notable and tragic lifeboat disasters which prompted the RNLI to set about improving still further the design of lifeboats.

In April 1947 the entire crew of the Mumbles lifeboat was lost as it went to the aid of the steamship *Santampa* off the South Wales coast. In February 1953 the lifeboat stationed at Fraserburgh in the north-east of Scotland was overwhelmed and capsized close to the harbour entrance; six of her seven crew were lost. Further capsizes occurred at Bridlington in 1952, Arbroath in 1953 and Scarborough in 1954, all with fatal consequences, and in November 1962 the 35½ foot (10.8 metre) Liverpool-type non-self-righting lifeboat in service at Seaham Harbour, County Durham, capsized only a stone's throw from the harbour pier, resulting in the loss of five of her crew.

As a result of these capsizes the RNLI reviewed its policy on self-righting lifeboats and increased its efforts to find a better design of lifeboat, which would minimise the risks to its crews. The situation that existed in the 1950s was the result of a combination of historical preferences and the inability to design a lifeboat that would self-right if capsized but also had a high degree of lateral stability to make capsize unlikely in the first place. This problem had challenged naval architects for well over a century and remained unsolved. The majority of the motor lifeboats that were built up to the mid 1960s were based on Watson's non-self-righting hull shape.

The 46 foot 9 inch (14.2 metre) Watson cabin motor lifeboat 'Herbert Leigh', built in 1951, served at Barrow until 1982. She was a standard Watson motor lifeboat and, although built for service more than half a century after George Watson's first designs,had a hull very close in shape to that of the first Watson sailing lifeboat built in 1890. After being taken out of service, 'Herbert Leigh' was placed on display at the Dock Museum in Barrow-in-Furness, where she can still be seen. (The Barrow News and Mail Ltd)

The 37 foot (11.3 metre) Oakley class lifeboat 'Bird's Eye' from New Quay in Cardiganshire, which was built in 1970 and served at New Quay until 1990. The first 37 foot Oakley entered service in 1958 and the last in 1971, during which time a total of twenty-six boats of the class were built. (RNLI)

The solution to the problem was provided by Richard Oakley, the RNLI's Consulting Naval Architect. In the 1950s he designed a lifeboat 37 feet (11.3 metres) long that employed a system of water ballast transfer that would right the boat in the event of a capsize. It also had a high degree of inherent stability and thus represented a significant technological advance. This design became known as the 37 foot Oakley class and entered service in 1958. It can be regarded as the first of the modern generation of self-righting motor lifeboats.

Although new self-righting lifeboats had been introduced, the non-self-righting lifeboats still in service were liable to capsize in very heavy seas, as occurred off the coast of Scotland at Longhope in 1969 and Fraserburgh in 1970, with tragic loss of life. The entire crew of eight from the Longhope boat were lost, while at Fraserburgh it was the second lifeboat disaster in less than two decades. The change to self-righting lifeboats thus became more urgent and the RNLI altered its building policy so that the entire fleet of offshore lifeboats would be self-righting by 1980. This would be achieved by an increase in the construction programme of self-righting lifeboats and by fitting Watson and Barnett lifeboats with airbags that would give a once-only self-righting capacity.

The 37 foot 6 inch (11.4 metre) Rother class lifeboat 'Harold Salvesen', which was stationed at Amble until 1986 and then served in the Relief Fleet. The Rother shared the same hull shape as the 37 foot (11.3 metre) Oakley but the boat's capacity to self-right was achieved through the large enclosed watertight superstructure which caused the boat to come upright if it was overturned. This method of self-righting became the standard for all lifeboats built after the mid 1970s. (Nicholas Leach)

Left: *The launch of the 'Matthew Simpson' lifeboat at Ramsey, Isle of Man. A haul-off warp was attached to the pier head next to the launch site, and, as the boat slid off the carriage, the crew hauled on this line and pulled the boat into deeper water. Once it was afloat, the crew could row the boat away from the beach. During the nineteenth century a haul-off warp was used at various stations to get the boat afloat, particularly if a strong on-shore wind was encountered. The carriage launch is the oldest method of launching, and many stations still practise it today. (Derek Page, RNLI Ramsey Branch)*

Right: *The 40 foot (12.2 metre) self-righting lifeboat 'Lucy Newbon' at the top of the wooden slipway at Selsey, West Sussex. Before the First World War, lifeboats that were launched down a slip-way, such as at Selsey, were often kept in the open at the top of a slip, with little protection from the elements. (Photograph by a Shoreline member)*

Left: *The recovery at low water of Ilfracombe's 12 metre Mersey class life-boat 'Spirit of Derbyshire'. The procedure for recovering a lifeboat on to a carriage is a complicated one. Once the lifeboat is hauled out of the water, numerous shore helpers are required to ensure the boat is balanced upright ready to be pulled on to the launching carriage. (Nicholas Leach)*

Right: *The 12 metre Mersey class life-boat 'Her Majesty The Queen' being hauled up the East Beach at Cromer following a practice launch. When the lifeboat house at the end of Cromer pier was demolished in 1996 to be replaced by a new and larger house in the same place, the station reverted, albeit temporarily, to carriage launching. (Paul Russell)*

THE INSHORE LIFEBOAT

Throughout the history of the RNLI there have been changes to the pattern of lifeboat coverage as the type of casualty has changed. Before the 1960s few people could afford yachts or motor boats, and sports such as wind-sailing and surfing were almost unknown. However, as incomes and leisure time increased during the 1960s, more people began using the sea for recreation. As a result, lifeboats were called to an increasing number of inshore incidents. The conventional lifeboats were not well suited to such work and it was clear that simple, fast rescue craft were required for working inshore.

The 16 foot (4.9 metre) D class inflatable lifeboat D-362 'Kensington Rescuer' at Sheerness, Kent. Manned by a crew of two or three, this is one of the lifeboats that covers the busy Thames estuary. Small inflatable inshore lifeboats such as this were first introduced by the RNLI in 1963 and now form an essential part of the lifeboat service, saving many lives each year. (Nicholas Leach)

The RNLI bought an inflatable boat in 1962 for extensive trials, and a delegation visited France, where similar boats were in operation, to obtain further advice and see the boats in service. Following these initial steps, the first inshore rescue boats were introduced during the summer of 1963, when eight were sent to stations around Britain. Such was their success that each year more stations began to operate the boats. By 1966 the number of inshore rescue boats on station had risen to seventy-two, of which thirty-two remained on station throughout the year, the rest operating only during the summer. Some stations that had been established during the nine-

The inshore lifeboat house at Penarth in South Wales was built in 1995-6 to accommodate two inshore lifeboats: an Atlantic 75 and a D class inflatable. Since the 1980s the RNLI has embarked on a programme of modernising its shore facilities, and this has resulted in many new lifeboat houses being constructed, of which Penarth is one. The modern lifeboat houses incorporate sophisticated facilities for the crew; most new houses have training rooms, warm showers and good crew changing facilities, as well as workshop space to enable the crews to maintain the lifeboats to the highest standards and, if necessary, repair minor damage. Many houses are also built with a souvenir shop to sell the RNLI's wide range of gifts. (Nicholas Leach)

teenth century but closed following the advent of the motor lifeboat were reopened to operate an inshore lifeboat (ILB), as the new craft became known. At other places the ILBs were used to complement the existing offshore lifeboat and perform work close to the shore.

The 16 foot (4.9 metre) inflatable lifeboats, made from tough nylon with neoprene, had a crew of two. They were powered by a 40 horsepower outboard engine and could be launched quickly and easily. Their advantages were their speed, which at 20 knots was considerably faster than any other lifeboat in service during the 1960s; the ability to go alongside other craft or persons in the water without causing or suffering damage; the short time taken to launch; and the low running costs.

The inshore lifeboats were, and still are, hugely successful and carry out a great many rescues every year. However, by the late 1960s there was a requirement for a larger inshore lifeboat, capable of night operation and greater range, but retaining the advantages of the standard inshore lifeboat. After various rigid hulls had been tested, one developed at Atlantic College in South Wales was deemed the most suitable. The new boat had a rigid wooden hull with inflatable sponsons attached to it, to give the boat great stability, and was fitted with twin outboard engines, which enabled a speed of over 30 knots to be achieved. Named the Atlantic 21, the new model was developed and refined by the RNLI, and in 1972 the first of the class was stationed at Hartlepool. The advantages of the design soon became apparent, and more and more stations now operate Atlantic rigid-inflatables. The importance to the RNLI of these small, fast boats cannot be overstated.

New recovery of the Atlantic 21 at Sheringham, Norfolk, on to the drive-on drive-off launch carriage using a net. The lifeboat is driven straight into the open end of the carriage at speed and stopped by an arrester net; then the tractor hauls her clear of the water before a following wave arrives. This method of recovery is used if the lifeboat needs to be landed from the water quickly. (Paul Russell)

The Atlantic 75 B-711 'Helene' in rough seas off Bundoran, County Donegal. The Atlantic 75 is the successor to the Atlantic 21 and is the fastest design of lifeboat the RNLI currently operates. There are many Atlantics on station, and lifeboat crews have performed some notable services using their speed, manoeuvrability and versatility, which combine to make them excellent rescue craft. (Nicholas Leach)

19

Above left: *The prototype 44 foot (13.4 metre) Waveney 44-001 moored at Harwich on temporary relief duty. The Waveney class was developed during the 1960s from a rescue cutter designed by the United States Coastguard for use in America. The RNLI bought one in the mid 1960s and numbered it 44-001 (designating its length and that it was the first of the class). After extensive trials around the British coast, they started building boats of the same design. (Nicholas Leach)*

Above right: *The 44 foot (13.4 metre) Waveney 'Barham', stationed at Great Yarmouth and Gorleston, leaves the harbour entrance. The Waveney was a radical departure from the conventional displacement hulled motor lifeboats in service until the 1980s. It had a semi-planing hull, which partly lifted from the water at speed, enabling it to achieve 15 knots, almost twice the speed of the lifeboats then in service. As the RNLI's first 'fast' lifeboat, it pointed the way for future lifeboat design and a total of twenty-two Waveneys were eventually built, the last in 1982. (Nicholas Leach)*

INTO THE TWENTY-FIRST CENTURY

During the 1960s further developments in lifeboat design took place. Following the International Lifeboat Conference at Edinburgh in 1963, the RNLI purchased a 44 foot (13.4 metre) steel-hulled lifeboat from the United States Coastguard service for trials around Britain. This boat, self-righting by virtue of its watertight wheelhouse, was faster than the conventional lifeboats then in service and completely different from the traditional British lifeboat designs. The American boat, numbered 44-001 by the RNLI, was taken on a tour of stations throughout the British Isles. The reaction of lifeboat crews to the new design was so favourable that a building programme was embarked upon. The type was given the class name Waveney, and it was the first of the modern generation of 'fast' lifeboats.

The Waveney lifeboat, capable of over 14 knots, was highly successful, and the boats were well liked at the stations where they operated. But with the demands on its lifeboats always changing, by the late 1960s the RNLI believed that a slightly larger and faster lifeboat was needed, so a new 52 foot (15.8 metre) type was designed and built. This was the Arun class, and it has proved to be one of the finest lifeboat types ever developed for use by the RNLI. Capable of a speed between 18 and

The first 52 foot (15.8 metre) Arun class life-boat to be built, named 'Arun', and stationed for most of her service life at Barry Dock in South Wales. She was built in wood, unlike later boats that were moulded from glass-reinforced plastic. The straight deck made it difficult to pull people out of the water, and this, as well as the experimental wheelhouse and superstructure, was changed in later boats of the same class. (Nicholas Leach)

Left: The 52 foot (15.8 metre) Arun class lifeboat 'Charles Brown', stationed at Buckie, with Coxswain John Murray at the helm. She was built in 1984. The Arun has proved to be one of the RNLI's most successful designs of all-weather lifeboat and won a Design Council award in 1982. Forty-six of the Arun class were built. (Nicholas Leach)

Right: The 12 metre (38 foot) Mersey class lifeboat 'Frank and Lena Clifford of Stourbridge', stationed at New Quay, Wales. The Mersey was designed for stations that practised carriage launching. The propellers were protected by bilge keels and partial tunnels so that when the boat was beached they would not be damaged. (Gilbert Hampton Photography, courtesy of the RNLI)

Right: Lowestoft's 47 foot (14.3 metre) Tyne class lifeboat 'Spirit of Lowestoft' is kept afloat, although the Tyne class, introduced in 1982, was designed to be slipway-launched. The boat has a low wheelhouse to enable it to fit inside boat-houses, and propellers fully protected by substantial bilge keels running along the hull. Lowestoft station provides cover for the notorious sandbanks off the coast of East Anglia, and the protected propellers of the Tyne class ensure that the boat can take the ground without damage. (Paul Russell)

20 knots, the Arun was completely different from any previous lifeboat design. Its speed enabled it to reach casualties more quickly, so reducing the chances of the situation deteriorating and making a rescue more difficult.

The introduction of the Waveney and Arun 'fast' lifeboats in the 1960s and 1970s marked the beginning of the modernisation undertaken by the RNLI, and during the 1980s further improvements were effected. Two new classes of 'fast' lifeboat were introduced: the 47 foot (14.3 metre) Tyne class and the 12 metre Mersey class, intended for stations which practised slipway and carriage launching. In addition, several completely new stations were established, including a number on the west coast of Ireland. In 1980 this part of the coast was served by just three offshore lifeboats, but by 1996 six offshore and five inshore lifeboat stations were operational – a significant improvement in coverage.

The change-over of lifeboats at Hoylake: the 12 metre Mersey lifeboat 'Lady of Hilbre' replaced the 37 foot 6 inch (11.4 metre) Rother lifeboat 'Mary Gabriel' in October 1990. The Mersey class replaced lifeboats of the 37 foot (11.3 metre) Oakley and 37 foot 6 inch Rother classes. (Nicholas Leach)

The 46 foot (14 metre) Trent class lifeboat 'Frederick Storey Cockburn' stationed at Courtmacsherry Harbour on the south coast of Ireland. The Trent is one of two new classes of fast lifeboats designed to lie afloat, capable of speeds of up to 25 knots. (Gilbert Hampton Photography, courtesy of the RNLI)

The Severn class are the RNLI's most modern lifeboats; at 17 metres (55 feet 9 inches), they are one of the largest designs ever built and, together with the Trent, are the fastest. This particular boat, 'Pride of the Humber', operates from the Humber station at Spurn Point, at the mouth of the river Humber, and is manned by the only full-time lifeboat crew in Britain. Because of the isolated location and the frequency with which the lifeboat is needed, the entire crew are full-time employees of the RNLI and live at Spurn with their families. (Nicholas Leach)

The number of launches performed by the RNLI's lifeboats has increased rapidly since the Second World War, particularly since the introduction of the inshore lifeboat in 1963. In 1947 lifeboats were launched on service 588 times and saved 427 lives. During the 1970s and 1980s, however, lifeboats were launched more than 2500 times on service each year, and this figure has continued to rise: in 1990 there were 4946 service launches by lifeboats and in 1995 there were 7312 launches.

While the demand for the RNLI's services increased considerably during the last two decades of the twentieth century, perhaps the most significant development was the increase in the speed of lifeboats themselves and the resulting reduction in time taken to reach casualties. In 1986 a target date of 1993 was set by when it was intended to have fast lifeboats operating from every station equipped with an all-weather lifeboat. Faster all-weather lifeboats became the norm, and the RNLI extended its declared area of coverage from 30 miles (48 km) to 50 miles (80 km) offshore. The change to the fast lifeboats, of which the Waveney was the first, is as significant a development as the introduction of the motor lifeboat during the first half of the twentieth century. As the RNLI prepares for the twenty-first century, not only are all offshore lifeboats capable of at least 14 knots, but a new generation of even faster lifeboats is being built and the boats are entering service. The Trent and Severn classes can reach speeds of 25 knots and operate in the worst of weathers, ensuring that the RNLI maintains its tradition of providing a comprehensive sea rescue service.

The self-righting trial of the 47 foot (14.3 metre) Tyne class lifeboat 'Sir William Hillary' at Cowes. All modern lifeboats undergo trials like this shortly after being built, to ensure that they will right as designed in an emergency. Several modern lifeboats have been capsized on service and righted successfully. The Waveney class lifeboat 'The Scout', stationed at Hartlepool, capsized twice on service to the tanker 'Freja Svea' in February 1993 and righted on both occasions. Although one lifeboatman was washed overboard during the capsizes he was recovered, and the whole crew reached port safely with only a few injuries. (Gilbert Hampton Photography, courtesy of the RNLI)

The naming ceremony of a new lifeboat is a proud occasion for the community in which the lifeboat will serve. During the formal ceremony, at which the local vicar performs the dedication of the lifeboat, the Lifeboat Hymn, 'For those in peril on the sea', is sung. After this, the lifeboat is named, usually by the donor, and a champagne bottle broken over her bow, accompanied by the traditional words 'God bless her and all who sail in her'. These photographs show new lifeboats being named at Dun Laoghaire in October 1938 (left), Lytham St Anne's in May 1990 (below left) and Blyth in July 1996 (below right). (Photographs: Dun Laoghaire, RNLI; Lytham and Blyth, Nicholas Leach)

STATIONS AND CREWS

The lifeboats that protect the coasts of the United Kingdom and the Republic of Ireland are fast and seaworthy craft, but they are only as good as the men and women who operate them. The crews have always been volunteers, who willingly give up their time for service calls, exercises, training and the day to day running of the station. They come from all walks of life and are willing to exchange the comfort of their homes for the danger and discomfort of saving lives at sea. Usually the only full-time member of the crew at an all-weather lifeboat station is the mechanic, whose job it is to maintain the lifeboat and its gear. There is one completely full-time crew, at the busy Humber station in East Yorkshire, where the men and their families live on the isolated Spurn Point peninsula.

The crew of the 'Mary Isabella' lifeboat at Ramsey, Isle of Man, in the 1890s. Coxswain Robert Garrett is seated in the front row, centre right. (Derek Page, RNLI Ramsey Branch)

Each of the RNLI's lifeboat stations operates with a degree of autonomy but under the regulations and supervision of the Institution. Each station has an honorary secretary, who is responsible for the running of the station. The Coastguard are usually the first people to know about a casualty, and if a lifeboat is needed they will contact the honorary secretary to request the launch of the lifeboat. The volunteer crew are alerted by pagers, telephone or maroons, and they will immediately leave what they are doing, whether at home or at work, and make for the lifeboat station. Often a lifeboat will be at sea in less than four minutes from the time the crew was alerted. Once the boat is at sea, the coxswain or helmsman is in sole charge of it and will make the decisions about how best to tackle the rescue which faces the lifeboat and its crew.

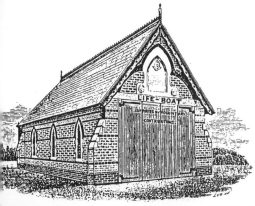

Left: *The 'standard' lifeboat house of the nineteenth century was designed by C. H. Cooke, who was appointed Honorary Architect to the RNLI in 1857. By the 1870s many lifeboat houses had been built to his plans. The lifeboat house is as much a part of any lifeboat station as the lifeboat, and former lifeboat houses can be seen at many places, put to a variety of uses. Despite the existence of a standard design in the nineteenth century, boathouses were very different, with their own unique setting and architecture. Since 1900 boathouses have not been built to a standard design; some are functional and bland in appearance, while others are more ornamental, incorporating decorative features. (From an original engraving published in 1874.)*

Above: *The old lifeboat house at Solva, Pembrokeshire, was built in 1869 on ground given by Trinity House and used until the station closed in 1887. The original stone tablet commemorating the donor can still be seen on the outside wall. (Nicholas Leach)*

Below: *The lifeboat house and slipway at Tenby, Pembrokeshire, were built in 1905 and have been modified, adapted and strengthened several times since to make them suitable for housing new lifeboats that have been sent to the station. The slipway, at 366 feet (112 metres) in length, is one of the longest in Britain. (Nicholas Leach)*

Above: *At Aberystwyth the lifeboat house built in 1875 to Cooke's design was used until the offshore lifeboat was withdrawn from the station in 1964. It has been little altered externally and is now used by BBC Wales. (Nicholas Leach)*

Below: *One of the RNLI's most modern lifeboat houses is at Angle, Pembrokeshire. It was built in 1991-2 at a cost of over £1 million and replaced a boathouse on the same site that had deteriorated to such an extent that it was deemed beyond economical repair. (Nicholas Leach)*

LIFEBOAT STATIONS IN GREAT BRITAIN AND IRELAND

This gazetteer lists the places where an RNLI lifeboat station is currently operational. It is arranged geographically, clockwise round the coast of Great Britain from Northumberland to Borders, and clockwise round the Irish coast from Antrim to Donegal. The Channel Islands will be found between South Devon and Cornwall, and the Isle of Man between Scotland and Ireland. The name and type of each lifeboat, as on 31st January 1998, are given though as new boats go on station this information will become out of date.

GREAT BRITAIN AND CHANNEL ISLANDS

NORTHUMBERLAND
Berwick-upon-Tweed: 12m Mersey, *Joy and Charles Beeby*; D class inflatable.
North Sunderland: 12m Mersey, *Grace Darling*; D class inflatable.
Craster: D class inflatable.
Amble: 44ft Waveney, *Margaret Graham*; D class inflatable.
Newbiggin: Atlantic 21, *Kirklees*.
Blyth: 14m Trent *Windsor Runner (Civil Service No.42)*; D class inflatable.
Cullercoats: Atlantic 21, *Edmund and Joan White*.
Tynemouth: 52ft Arun, *George and Olive Turner*; D class inflatable.

DURHAM
Sunderland: 14m Trent, *Macquarie*; D class inflatable.
Hartlepool: 47ft Tyne, *City of Sheffield*; Atlantic 21, *Burton Brewer*.

YORKSHIRE
Teesmouth: 47ft Tyne, *Phil Mead*.
Redcar: Atlantic 21, *Leicester Challenge*; D class inflatable.
Staithes and Runswick: Atlantic 21, *Ellis Sinclair*.
Whitby: 14m Trent, *George and Mary Webb*; D class inflatable.
Scarborough: 12m Mersey, *Fanny Victoria Wilkinson and Frank Stubbs*; D class inflatable.
Filey: 12m Mersey, *Keep Fit Association*; D class inflatable.
Flamborough: Atlantic 75, *Jason Logg*.
Bridlington: 12m Mersey, *Marine Engineer*; D class inflatable.
Withernsea: D class inflatable.
Humber: 17m Severn, *Pride of the Humber*.

LINCOLNSHIRE
Cleethorpes: D class inflatable.
Mablethorpe: D class inflatable.
Skegness: 12m Mersey, *Lincolnshire Poacher*; D class inflatable.

NORFOLK
Hunstanton: Atlantic 21, *Spirit of America*.
Wells: 12m Mersey, *Doris M. Mann of Ampthill*; D class inflatable.
Sheringham: Atlantic 75, *Manchester Unity of Oddfellows*.
Cromer: 47ft Tyne, *Ruby and Arthur Reed II*; D class inflatable.
Happisburgh: D class inflatable.
Gorleston: 14m Trent, *Samarbeta*; Atlantic 21, *Joseph B. Press*.

SUFFOLK
Lowestoft: 47ft Tyne, *Spirit of Lowestoft*.
Southwold: Atlantic 21, *The Quiver*.
Aldeburgh: 12m Mersey, *Freddie Cooper*; D class inflatable.

ESSEX
Harwich: 17m Severn, *Albert Brown*; Atlantic 21, *British Diver II*.
Walton and Frinton: 47ft Tyne, *Kenneth Thelwall II*.
Clacton-on-Sea: Atlantic 21, *Institute of London Underwriters*; D class inflatable.
West Mersea: Atlantic 21, *Himley Hall*.
Burnham-on-Crouch: Atlantic 75, *Brandy Hole*; D class inflatable.
Southend-on-Sea: Atlantic 21, *Percy Garon II*; D class inflatable.

KENT
Sheerness: 14m Trent, *George and Ivy Swanson*; D class inflatable.
Whitstable: Atlantic 21, *British Diver*.

Margate: 12m Mersey, *Leonard Kent*; D class inflatable.
Ramsgate: 14m Trent, *Esme Anderson*; Atlantic 21, *Ramsgate Enterprise*.
Walmer: Atlantic 21, *James Burgess*.
Dover: 17m Severn, *City of London II*.
Littlestone-on-Sea: Atlantic 21, *The Lady Dart and Long Life II*.
Dungeness: 12m Mersey, *Pride and Spirit*.

SUSSEX
Rye Harbour: Atlantic 75, *Commander and Mrs Rodney Wells*.
Hastings: 12m Mersey, *Sealink Endeavour*; D class inflatable.
Eastbourne: 12m Mersey, *Royal Thames*; D class inflatable.
Newhaven: 52ft Arun, *Keith Anderson*.
Brighton: Atlantic 21, *Graham Hillier and Tony Cater*.
Shoreham Harbour: 47ft Tyne, *Hermione Lady Colwyn*; D class inflatable.
Littlehampton: Atlantic 21, *Blue Peter I*.
Selsey: 47ft Tyne, *City of London*; D class inflatable.

HAMPSHIRE AND THE ISLE OF WIGHT
Hayling Island: Atlantic 75, *Betty Battle*; D class inflatable.
Portsmouth: Atlantic 75, *CSMA Frizzell*; D class inflatable.
Bembridge: 47ft Tyne, *Max Aitken III*; D class inflatable.
Yarmouth: 52ft Arun, *Joy and John Wade*.
Calshot: 33ft Brede, *Safeway*.
Lymington: Atlantic 21, *Frank and Mary Atkinson*.

DORSET
Mudeford: Atlantic 21, *Ken Derham*.
Poole: 33ft Brede, *Inner Wheel*; Atlantic 75, *Friendly Forester II*.
Swanage: 12m Mersey, *Robert Charles Brown*; D class inflatable.
Weymouth: 54ft Arun, *Tony Vandervell*; Atlantic 21.
Lyme Regis: Atlantic 75, *Pearl of Dorset*.

SOUTH DEVON
Exmouth: 14m Trent, *Forward Birmingham*; D class inflatable.
Teignmouth: Atlantic 21, *Frank and Dorothy*.
Torbay: 52ft Arun, *Marie Winstone*; D class inflatable.
Salcombe: 47ft Tyne, *The Baltic Exchange II*.

Plymouth: 52ft Arun, *City of Plymouth*.

CHANNEL ISLANDS
Alderney: 14m Trent, *Roy Barker I*; D class inflatable.
St Peter Port: 17m Severn, *Spirit of Guernsey*.
St Helier: 47ft Tyne, *Alexander Coutanche*.
St Catherines: Atlantic 21, *Jessie Eliza*.

CORNWALL AND THE SCILLY ISLES
Looe: D class inflatable.
Fowey: 14m Trent, *Maurice and Joyce Hardy*; D class inflatable.
Falmouth: 17m Severn, *The Will*; Atlantic 21, *Falmouth Round Table*.
The Lizard: 47ft Tyne, *David Robinson*.
Marazion: D class inflatable.
Penlee: 52ft Arun, *Mabel Alice*.
Sennen Cove: 47ft Tyne, *Norman Salvesen*; D class inflatable.
St Mary's (Scilly): 17m Trent, *The Whiteheads*.
St Ives: 12m Mersey, *Princess Royal* (*Civil Service No.41*); D class inflatable.
St Agnes: D class inflatable.
Newquay: Atlantic 75, *Phyllis*; D class inflatable.
Padstow: 47ft Tyne, *James Burrough*.
Rock: D class inflatable.
Port Isaac: D class inflatable.
Bude: D class inflatable.

NORTH DEVON
Clovelly: Atlantic 21.
Appledore: Atlantic 75.
Ilfracombe: 12m Mersey, *Spirit of Derbyshire*; D class inflatable.

SOMERSET
Minehead: Atlantic 75, *Bessie*; D class inflatable.
Weston-super-Mare: Atlantic 21, *Weston Centenary*; D class inflatable.

WALES
Penarth: Atlantic 75, *Spirit of Penarth*; D class inflatable.
Barry Dock: 52ft Arun, *Margaret Frances Love*.
Atlantic College: Atlantic 21, *American Ambassador*.
Porthcawl: Atlantic 75, *Giles*.
Port Talbot: D class inflatable.
The Mumbles: 47ft Tyne, *Ethel Anne Measures*; D class inflatable.
Horton and Port Eynon: D class inflatable.

Burry Port: D class inflatable.
Tenby: 47ft Tyne, *RFA Sir Galahad*; D class inflatable.
Angle: 47ft Tyne, *The Lady Rank*; D class inflatable.
Little and Broad Haven: D class inflatable.
St David's: 47ft Tyne, *Garside;* D class inflatable.
Fishguard: 14m Trent, *Blue Peter VII*; D class inflatable.
Cardigan: C class inflatable.
New Quay: 12m Mersey, *Frank and Lena Clifford of Stourbridge*; D class inflatable.
Aberystwyth: Atlantic 75, *Enid Mary*.
Borth: D class inflatable.
Aberdovey: Atlantic 21, *Long Life III*.
Barmouth: 12m Mersey, *Moira Barrie*; D class inflatable.
Criccieth: Atlantic 75, *Mercurius*.
Pwllheli: 12m Mersey, *Lilly and Vincent Anthony*; D class inflatable.
Abersoch: Atlantic 21, *Borough of Solihull*.
Porthdinllaen: 47ft Tyne, *Hetty Rampton*.
Trearddur Bay: Atlantic 75, *Dorothy Selina*.
Holyhead: 47ft Tyne, *St Cybi II* (*Civil Service No.40*); D class inflatable.
Moelfre: 47ft Tyne, *Robert and Violet*; D class inflatable.
Beaumaris: Atlantic 21, *Blue Peter II*.
Conwy: D class inflatable.
Llandudno: 12m Mersey, *Andy Pearce*; D class inflatable.
Rhyl: 12m Mersey, *Lil Cunningham*; D class inflatable.
Flint: D class inflatable.

CHESHIRE
West Kirby: D class inflatable.
Hoylake: 12m Mersey, *Lady of Hilbre*.
New Brighton: Atlantic 75, *Rock Light*.

LANCASHIRE
Lytham St Anne's: 47ft Tyne, *Sarah Emily Harrop*; D class inflatable.
Blackpool: Atlantic 75, *Rotaract I*; D class inflatable.
Fleetwood: 47ft Tyne, *William Street*; D class inflatable.
Morecambe: D class inflatable.

CUMBRIA
Barrow: 47ft Tyne, *James Bibby*; D class inflatable.
St Bees: Atlantic 75, *Percy Henry Patmore MBE MM*.
Workington: 47ft Tyne, *Sir John Fisher*.

Silloth: Atlantic 75, *Spirit of Cumbria*.

DUMFRIES AND GALLOWAY
Kippford: D class inflatable.
Kirkcudbright: Atlantic 21, *Peter and Grace Ewing*.
Portpatrick: 47ft Tyne, *Mary Irene Millar*.
Stranraer: D class inflatable.

STRATHCLYDE
Girvan: 12m Mersey, *Silvia Burrell*.
Troon: 52ft Arun, *City of Glasgow III*.
Largs: Atlantic 75.
Helensburgh: Atlantic 21, *Andrew Mason*.
Tighnabruaich: Atlantic 21, *Blenwatch*.
Arran (Lamlash): C class inflatable.
Campbeltown: 52ft Arun, *Walter and Margaret Couper*; D class inflatable.
Oban: 14m Trent, *Mora Edith Macdonald*.
Tobermory: 54ft Arun, *City of Bradford IV*.
Islay: 17m Severn, *Helmut Schroder of Dunlossit II*.

WESTERN ISLES
Barra Island: 52ft Arun, *Ann Lewis Fraser*.
Stornoway: 52ft Arun, *Sir Max Aitken II*.

HIGHLAND
Mallaig: 52ft Arun, *The Davina and Charles Matthews Hunter*.
Kyle of Lochalsh: Atlantic 75, *Alexander Cattanach*.
Portree: 14m Trent, *Stanley Watson Barker*.
Lochinver: 52ft Arun, *Murray Lornie*.

ORKNEY
Longhope: 47ft Tyne, *Lord Saltoun*.
Kirkwall: 52ft Arun, *Mickie Salvesen*.
Stromness: 52ft Arun, *Joseph Rothwell Sykes and Hilda M*.

SHETLAND
Lerwick: 17m Severn, *Michael and Jane Vernon*.
Aith: 52ft Arun, *Snolda*.

HIGHLAND
Thurso: 52ft Arun, *The Queen Mother*.
Wick: 14m Trent, *Roy Barker II*.
Invergordon: 14m Trent, *Douglas Aikman Smith*.
North Kessock: D class inflatable.

GRAMPIAN
Buckie: 52ft Arun, *Charles Brown*.
Macduff: Atlantic 21, *The Rotary Club of Glasgow*.
Fraserburgh: 47ft Tyne, *City of Edinburgh*.

Peterhead: 47ft Tyne, *Babs and Agnes Robertson.*
Aberdeen: 54ft Arun, *BP Forties*; D class inflatable.

TAYSIDE
Montrose: 47ft Tyne, *Moonbeam*; D class inflatable.
Arbroath: 12m Mersey, *Inchcape*; D class inflatable.
Broughty Ferry: 52ft Arun, *Spirit of Tayside*; D class inflatable.

FIFE
Anstruther: 12m Mersey, *Kingdom of Fife.*
Kinghorn: Atlantic 75, *Frederick Robertson.*

LOTHIAN
Queensferry: Atlantic 75, *Donald and Ethel Macrae.*
North Berwick: D class inflatable.
Dunbar: 14m Trent, *Sir Ronald Pechell Bt*; D class inflatable.

BORDERS
St Abbs: Atlantic 21, *Dorothy and Katherine Barr.*
Eyemouth: 14m Trent, *Barclaycard Crusader.*

ISLE OF MAN
Ramsey: 12m Mersey, *Ann and James Ritchie.*
Douglas: 47ft Tyne, *Sir William Hillary.*
Port St Mary: 54ft Arun, *The Gough-Ritchie*; D class inflatable.
Port Erin: Atlantic 21, *Herbert and Edith.*
Peel: 12m Mersey, *Ruby Clery.*

IRELAND

CO. ANTRIM
Portrush: 52ft Arun, *Richard Evans* (*Civil Service No.39*); D class inflatable.
Red Bay: Atlantic 75, *Dorothy Mary.*
Larne: 44ft Waveney, *The William and Jane*; D class inflatable.

CO. DOWN
Bangor: Atlantic 21, *Youth of Ulster.*
Donaghadee: 52ft Arun, *City of Belfast.*
Portaferry: Atlantic 75, *Blue Peter V.*
Newcastle: 12m Mersey, *Eleanor and Bryant Girling*; D class inflatable.
Kilkeel: Atlantic 21, *Valerie Hull.*

CO. LOUTH
Clogher Head: 12m Mersey, *Doris Bleasdale.*

CO. DUBLIN
Skerries: Atlantic 21.
Howth: 52ft Arun, *City of Dublin*; D class inflatable.
Dun Laoghaire: 14m Trent, *Anna Livia*; D class inflatable.

CO. WICKLOW
Wicklow: 47ft Tyne, *Annie Blaker*; D class inflatable.
Arklow: 14m Trent, *Ger Tigchelaar.*
Courtown: D class inflatable.

CO. WEXFORD
Rosslare Harbour: 52ft Arun, *St Brendan.*
Kilmore Quay: 12m Mersey, *Mary Margaret.*
Fethard: D class inflatable.

CO. WATERFORD
Dunmore East: 14m Trent, *Elizabeth and Ronald.*
Tramore: D class inflatable.
Helvick Head: Atlantic 21.

CO. CORK
Youghal: Atlantic 21, *Marjory Turner.*
Ballycotton: 52ft Arun, *Hyman Winstone.*
Courtmacsherry Harbour: 14m Trent, *Frederick Storey Cockburn.*
Baltimore: 47ft Tyne, *Hilda Jarrett.*
Castletownbere: 52ft Arun, *Roy and Barbara Harding.*

CO. KERRY
Valentia: 17m Severn, *John and Margaret Doig.*
Fenit: 52ft Arun, *Ralph and Bonella Farrant.*

CO. CLARE
Kilrush: Atlantic 75, *Rose West.*

CO. GALWAY
Aran Islands: 17m Trent, *David Kirkaldy.*
Galway: Atlantic 75, *Dochas.*
Clifden: C class inflatable.

CO. MAYO
Achill: 52ft Arun, *Soldian.*
Ballyglass: 52ft Arun, *Mabel Williams.*

CO. DONEGAL
Bundoran: Atlantic 75, *Helene.*
Arranmore: 47ft Tyne, *William Luckin.*
Lough Swilly: Atlantic 75, *Daisy Aitken*; D class inflatable.

WHERE TO SEE OLD LIFEBOATS

This list includes those places where actual lifeboats can be seen on display. There are many other museums and centres where lifeboat-related material can be seen.

Bamburgh. The Grace Darling Museum, 1 Radcliffe Road, Bamburgh, Northumberland NE69 7AE. Telephone: 01668 214465. Items relating to Grace Darling, and a replica of the coble used in the rescue of the steamship *Forfarshire.*

Barrow-in-Furness. Dock Museum, North Road, Barrow-in-Furness, Cumbria LA14 2PU. Telephone: 01229 870871. The former Barrow lifeboat *Herbert Leigh* is displayed outside the museum.

Blackgang. Blackgang Sawmill and St Catherine's Quay, Blackgang, near Ventnor, Isle of Wight PO38 2HN. Telephone: 01983 730330. The former Flamborough lifeboat *Friendly Forester* is on display.

Buckie. Buckie Drifter, Fireuchny Road, Buckie, Banffshire AB56 1TT. Telephone: 01542 834646. The former Anstruther lifeboat *The Doctors* is on display outside.

Cardiff. Welsh Industrial and Maritime Museum, Bute Street, Cardiff CF1 6AN. Telephone: 01222 481919. The former Moelfre lifeboat *Watkin Williams,* in which a Gold Medal rescue was performed, is displayed outside.

Charlestown. Shipwreck and Heritage Museum, Charlestown, near St Austell, Cornwall PL25 2NT. Telephone: 01726 69897.

The former Scarborough lifeboat *Amelia* is on display outside.

Chatham. Chatham Historic Dockyard, Chatham, Kent ME4 4TE. Telephone: 01634 812551. The home of the National Lifeboat Collection, which consists of the following lifeboats: the first 37ft Oakley lifeboat, *J. G. Graves of Sheffield;* the former Holyhead lifeboat *St Cybi (Civil Service No.9);* former Sennen Cove lifeboat *Susan Ashley;* the former Torbay lifeboat *Edward Bridges (C.S. & P.O. No.37);* the former North Sunderland and Youghal lifeboat *Grace Darling;* the unique 28ft Harbour class lifeboat *Helen Blake;* the former Margate lifeboat *North Foreland (Civil Service No.11);* the former Yarmouth and Falmouth lifeboat *B.A.S.P.;* the last Flamborough lifeboat *The Will and Fanny Kirby;* the prototype 44ft Waveney 44-001; and the pulling lifeboats *Lizzie Porter, St Paul* and *James Leath.* There are also displays relating to the history of lifeboats and the RNLI.

Cromer. Cromer Lifeboat Museum, The Gangway, Cromer, Norfolk. Telephone: 01263 512503. The centrepiece is the former Cromer lifeboat *H. F. Bailey,* in which Coxswain Henry Blogg performed some notable medal-winning rescues. There are many

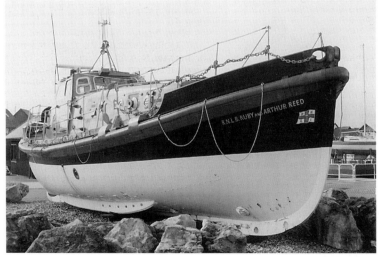

The 48 foot 6 inch (14.8 metre) Oakley lifeboat 'Ruby and Arthur Reed' on display at Hythe Marina, Southampton. (Nicholas Leach)

other items relating to the Cromer station and the exploits of Blogg.

Donaghadee, County Down. The former Donaghadee lifeboat *Sir Samuel Kelly*, on loan from the Ulster Folk and Transport Museum, is on display close to the harbour.

Dublin. The former Ballycotton lifeboat *Mary Stanford* is displayed at the Grand Canal Basin.

Dudley. The former Selsey lifeboat *Charles Henry* is displayed outside Merry Hill Shopping Centre at Waterfront Way.

Duxford. Imperial War Museum, Duxford Airfield, Cambridge CB2 4QR. Telephone: 01223 835000. The fully restored former Bembridge lifeboat *Jesse Lumb* is on display in a hanger.

Gorleston-on-Sea, Norfolk. The former Great Yarmouth and Gorleston lifeboat *John and Mary Meiklam of Gladswood* is displayed inside the lifeboat house.

Hartlepool. The former Filey lifeboat *Robert and Dorothy Hardcastle* is kept at the power station and used for display and fund-raising purposes in the north-east.

Harwich. Lifeboat Museum, Timberfields, off Wellington Road, Harwich, Essex CO12 3TE. Telephone: 01255 503429. The former Clacton lifeboat *Valentine Wyndham-Quin* is on display.

Holywood. Ulster Folk and Transport Museum, Cultra, Holywood, County Down BT18 0EU. Telephone: 01232 428428. The lifeboat *William and Laura* is in storage, not at present on display to the public.

Hythe, near Southampton. The former Cromer lifeboat *Ruby and Arthur Reed* is on display at the marina.

Irvine. Scottish Maritime Museum, Laird Forge Buildings, Gottries Road, Irvine, Ayrshire KA12 8QU. Telephone: 01294 278283. The former Longhope lifeboat *TGB* is on display; the pulling lifeboat *Jane Anne* is undergoing restoration for future display.

Kirkleatham. Kirkleatham Old Hall Museum, Kirkleatham, near Redcar TS10 5NW. Telephone: 01642 479500. The former Redcar lifeboat *Sir James Knott* is on display.

Land's End, Cornwall. Telephone: 01736 871501. The lifeboat *James and Catherine MacFarlane*, which served at the Lizard station in Cornwall, is on display outside the exhibitions complex.

Lower Basildon. Beale Park, Church Farm, Lower Basildon, Reading, Berkshire RG8 9NH. Telephone: 01734 845172. The former Newbiggin lifeboat *Mary Joicey* is displayed.

Lynmouth, Devon. The lifeboat *Docea Chapman*, renamed *Louisa II* to commemorate a famous overland launch which started in Lynmouth, is on display inside the tourist information centre.

Milford Haven. Outside on a launching carriage in the docks is *Calouste Gulbenkian*, an early 37ft Oakley class lifeboat.

Moelfre, Anglesey. The former New Quay lifeboat *Bird's Eye* is inside the Sea Watch Centre with a small display relating to the local lifeboats.

Oulton Broad, Lowestoft. In the car park of the International Boatbuilding Centre is the former Wells lifeboat *Ernest Tom Neathercoat*.

Pitsea. National Motorboat Museum, Wat Tyler Country Park, Pitsea, Basildon, Essex SS16 4UW. Telephone: 01268 550077. The former Wick lifeboat *Princess Marina* is on display.

Poole, Dorset. Displayed outside at the RNLI's depot is the first 48ft Oakley lifeboat, *The Earl and Countess Howe*. In the Old Lifeboat House on the Quay is the former Poole lifeboat *Thomas Kirk Wright.*

Porthleven, Cornwall. At the Shipwreck Centre is the former Blyth lifeboat *Dash* undergoing restoration for future display.

Redcar. Zetland Lifeboat Museum, 5 King Street, Redcar TS10 3PF. Telephone: 01642 486952. *Zetland*, the oldest lifeboat in the world still in existence, which was built by Henry Greathead in 1802; other exhibits relating to lifeboats at Redcar.

St David's, Pembrokeshire. Outside the Marine Life Centre is the former Rhyl lifeboat *Har-Lil.*

St Helier, Jersey. The lifeboat *Howard D* is undergoing restoration for display in Jersey.

Sheringham, Norfolk. The former Sheringham lifeboat *Foresters' Centenary* is undergoing restoration for future display as part of a lifeboat museum to be built in the town. On display is the fishermen's lifeboat *Henry Ramey Upcher*, built in 1894 and used at Sheringham until 1935.

South Shields. Near the bus terminus in Ocean Road is the *Tyne*, one of the oldest lifeboats in existence, under a small shelter close to a memorial to the lifeboat designers William Wouldhave and Henry Greathead.

Southwold, Suffolk. The former Southwold lifeboat *Alfred Corry* is undergoing restoration by the river Blyth for future display.

Swansea. Swansea Maritime and Industrial

31

Museum, Museum Square, Maritime Quarter, Swansea SA1 1SN. Telephone: 01792 470371 or 650351. The restored former Aberystwyth lifeboat *John and Naomi Beattie* and former Mumbles lifeboat *William Gammon – Manchester and District XXX*, together with an exhibition about lifeboats in Wales.

Weybourne. Muckleburgh Collection, Old Military Camp, Weybourne, Norfolk NR25 7EG. Telephone: 01263 588210. The former Sheringham lifeboats *J. C. Madge* and *Manchester Unity of Oddfellows* are on display, but there are plans to take them to Sheringham for display there.

Whitby. Lifeboat Museum, The Old Lifeboat House, Pier Road, Whitby, North Yorkshire. Telephone: 01947 602001. The last pulling lifeboat in active service, *Robert and Ellen Robson,* is displayed with other exhibits associated with the Whitby lifeboats.

For details of the other museums and display centres, as well as information about opening times of lifeboat stations, the RNLI produces an excellent *Lifeboat Stations and Museums Guide*, updated each year, available from their headquarters (address below).

ORGANISATIONS

Royal National Lifeboat Institution, West Quay Road, Poole, Dorset BH15 1HZ.

Lifeboat Enthusiasts' Society: membership details from Mrs Pam Francis, 13 West Way, Petts Wood, Orpington, Kent BR5 1LN.

Humber-Tees Lifeboat Research Group: membership details from John Fox, Ernest Cottages, 17 Lees Hall Road, Thornhill Lees, Dewsbury, West Yorkshire WF12 0RH.

Norfolk and Suffolk Research Group: membership details from Mark Roberts, 4 Paines Orchard, Cheddington, Buckinghamshire LU7 0SN.

North-West Research Group: membership details from John Tranter, 29 Ripon Road, Ansdell, Lytham St Anne's, Lancashire FY8 4DS.

Thames Estuary Research Group: membership details from Ron Fagance, 15 Old House Road, Balsham, Cambridge CB1 6EF.

FURTHER READING

This list contains the major works which should be consulted by those wishing to increase their knowledge of lifeboat history and development. There are, in addition, hundreds of booklets relating to specialist aspects of lifeboat history and individual lifeboat stations.

Beattie, John. *Lifeboats to the Rescue.* David & Charles, 1980.
Cockroft, Barry. *Fatal Call of the Running Tide.* Hodder & Stoughton, 1995.
Courcy Ireland, John de. *Wreck and Rescue on the East Coast of Ireland.* Glendale Press, Dublin, 1983.
Cumming, John. *Literature of the Life-boat 1785-1947.* RNLI, 1947.
Fry, Eric. *Lifeboat Design and Development.* David & Charles, 1975.
Howarth, Patrick. *The Lifeboat Story.* Routledge & Kegan Paul, 1957.
Howarth, Patrick. *Lifeboat in Danger's Hour.* Hamlyn, 1981.
Jolly, Cyril. *S.O.S. The Story of the Lifeboat Service.* Cassell, 1974.
Kipling, Ray. *Source Book of Lifeboats.* Ward Lock, 1974.
Kipling, Ray and Susannah. *Strong to Save.* Patrick Stephens, 1995.
Leach, Nicholas. *The Origins of the Lifeboat Service.* Published by the author, 1992.
Middleton, Eric. *Lifeboats of the World: A Pocket Encyclopaedia of Sea Rescue.* Blandford Press, 1977.
Wake-Walker, Edward. *RNLI Gold Medals.* RNLI, 1992.
Warner, Oliver. *The Lifeboat Service: A History of the Royal National Lifeboat Institution 1824-1974.* Cassell, 1974.